*Set design by Chris Pickart*

*Photo by Mark Garvin*

Jesse Bernstein, Mitchell Greenberg and Sam Henderson in a scene from the Arden Theatre Company/City Theatre production of *The Chosen*.

# THE CHOSEN

**ADAPTED BY AARON POSNER AND CHAIM POTOK**

From the novel by Chaim Potok

★

DRAMATISTS
PLAY SERVICE
INC.

THE CHOSEN was originally produced by the Arden Theatre Company (Terrence J. Nolen, Producing Artistic Director; Amy L. Murphy, Managing Director) in association with City Theatre (Marc Masterson, Artistic Director) in Philadelphia, Pennsylvania, on March 11, 1999. It was directed by Aaron Posner; the assistant director was Sladja Bukejlovic; the set design was by Chris Pickart; the lighting design was by James Leitner; the sound design was by Darron L. West and Kurt B. Kellenberger; the costume design was by Mimi O'Donnell; the dramaturg was Michele Osherow; the production manager was Matt Koropeckyj-Cox; and the production stage manager was Brady Gonsalves. The cast was as follows:

REUVEN MALTER and others ........... Michael Thomas Holmes
YOUNG REUVEN MALTER ........................... Jesse Bernstein
REB SAUNDERS ....................................... Mitchell Greenberg
DAVID MALTER ....................................................... Tom Teti
DANNY SAUNDERS ..................................... Sam Henderson

THE CHOSEN subsequently moved to City Theatre in Pittsburgh, Pennsylvania, on April 23, 1999. Patti Kelly replaced Brady Gonsalves as production stage manager.

# CHARACTERS

REUVEN MALTER
YOUNG REUVEN MALTER
REB SAUNDERS
DAVID MALTER
DANNY SAUNDERS
MR. GALANTER
DR. NATHAN APPLEMAN
JACK ROSE

# PLACE

Various locations in Williamsburg, Brooklyn.

# TIME

1944–48.

# THE CHOSEN

## ACT ONE

### Scene 1

### Reuven

*A large, open stage. There are two permanent locations: Malter's study and Saunders' office. There is a large open space in between and/or surrounding these two areas that is used for many other locations, including the baseball game/school yard, the hospital room, the street, the shul, and the rest. Scene changes should be kept as simple as possible so that the action can flow continuously between scenes with no breaks except by choice. Somewhere on the stage should be the presence of books, and somewhere there should be written, in Hebrew, the phrase "Ayloo ve'ayloo deevray eloheem chaiyeem." Translation: "Both these, and those, are the words of the living God."*

*Reuven enters. He is in his mid-thirties, a rabbi, a teacher, a thinker — a man of strong feelings and convictions and our guide for the evening. This is his story. He looks around at the offices, the theatre, the audience. He listens a moment ... Then, quietly, conscious of breaking the silence ...*

REUVEN. Silence. *(Pause.)* Silence. *(Pause.)* For a word to be spoken, there must be silence, both before and after. *(Beat.)* The

5

Zohar tells us, "Silence is good everywhere, except in connection with Torah." *(Brief pause. He thinks about this ... )* And the Talmud tells us that "A word is worth one coin; silence is worth two." *(Brief pause.)* The world I grew up in was not one of silence. *(Music plays and a collage of sound begins gently and grows — Williamsburg, Brooklyn, 1944. Foreign voices, laughter, street sounds, war news, children playing, music, city life, etc. ... )*

It was 1944, and while the war raged in Europe, Europe raged in Brooklyn. In our neighborhood alone you had Irish, Germans, Spanish (mostly refugees of the Spanish Civil War) and Jews from all over — including the Hasidim. *(Saunders enters, strolling through the streets of Brooklyn.)* There were three or four Hasidic courts in Williamsburg, each with their own synagogue, customs and fierce loyalties. They could be seen on the streets or behind shop counters, wearing their traditional garments of black and white, full beards, long earlocks (or *payos*), eking out meager livelihoods and dreaming of Shabbat and of festivals when they could close their shops and turn their attentions to their prayers, their rabbi and their God. *(Malter enters in a hurry, arms full of books, goes to his study.)*

I lived with my father — my mother had died when I was very young — and attended the yeshiva where he taught. Our apartment was small, and warm and crowded with books. In our home, words and ideas ... mattered. Mathematics was my first love. And Talmud. *(Realizing we may not know what the Talmud is.)* Oh. *(Explaining.)* The Talmud is the name for the books of Jewish Law that cover all areas of daily life from the preparation of food to the manner of prayer to the proper ways of conducting business. The Talmud was at the very center of all Jewish education, and, by tradition, virtuosity in the study of Talmud was considered the only true test of intellectual brilliance.

In addition to being a promising young Talmudist, however, I was also quite a good little pitcher and second baseman. *(Young Reuven jogs on in baseball outfit, ready for the game.)* I played on my yeshiva's team. A league had been organized the year before to prove to the gentile world that Jewish boys were actually "good Americans." *(Young Reuven says "good Americans" along with Reuven.)* That was important in 1944. I had, I remember particularly, a dropping curve that practically drove batters crazy.

*(Getting ready to launch into the story and the ball game.)* For the first sixteen years of our lives Danny Saunders and I lived within five blocks of each other and never knew of the other's existence. If it hadn't been for this new league, we probably never would have. You see, the Hasidic yeshiva that Danny attended organized a team, too, and one warm Sunday in June they showed up in our school yard for a game.

## Scene 2

## The Game

*Music plays. Danny enters, as though at the front of his team. We are at the baseball game in the school yard. We hear the sounds of the yard and throughout the game we hear the sounds of the crowds, the game, the cheering, the teams, etc.*

REUVEN. They were a unique sight. Fifteen boys in black and white, *payos* dangling, their fringes or *tzitzit* showing from beneath their shirts, and all with a look of grim determination. Our team wore whatever we wanted. A Hasidic rabbi sat on their bench, reading, hardly taking notice of the game. Our coach was our gym teacher, Mr. Galanter. *(He transforms himself into Mr. Galanter. Adds a hat, maybe ... )* He was a chunky man in his thirties with a very Semitic nose and a very wartime vocabulary. *(As Galanter, who barks rather than talks and wastes no words, but cares deeply for his boys and for this game:)*
REUVEN/GALANTER. Malter! Malter, get your *tuchus* over here!
REUVEN. *(As narrator.)* We all wondered, privately, why he wasn't off somewhere fighting in the war.
YOUNG REUVEN. Is everything okay, Mr. Galanter?
REUVEN/GALANTER. You're looking good out there, Malter. You got an arm like a sharpshooter.

7

YOUNG REUVEN. It'll be a good game.

REUVEN/GALANTER. A *tough* game. They're good little fighters.

YOUNG REUVEN. Those Hasidim?

REUVEN/GALANTER. Don't underestimate. They're killers. *(Reuven looks at Danny warming up. Not so impressive ... )*

YOUNG REUVEN. Really?

REUVEN/GALANTER. They play like winning is the first of the ten commandments. And they got Danny Saunders at first. Glue he's got in his glove — never misses a catch. His father is some big *macher* and he ordered them never to lose because it would shame the yeshiva or some *meshugunah* thing.

YOUNG REUVEN. Wow.

REUVEN/GALANTER. This Saunders, he hits hard, like a rocket the ball goes, and always right back at the pitcher. So stay alert at second. If you pitch later, be careful. I already told Shwartzie.

YOUNG REUVEN. Okay, Mr. Galanter. I'll watch out.

REUVEN/GALANTER. Good. Now, get out there. Okay, let's go, let's go, let's go! Keep the ranks close. Goldberg, move in. I could drive a battleship between you and Prosterman. That's it! Kantor, what are you looking for, paratroopers? Keep your head in the game!

DANNY. *(Yelling, in Yiddish.)* Gedenk talmidem far vemen un far voss mir shpielen!

REUVEN. *(Translating Danny's call.)* Remember for what and for whom we play ... Mr. Galanter was right: They were fierce. Their fielding was sloppy, their hitting uneven, but they were determined. Particularly Danny Saunders. He never missed a catch. And his first hit was a line drive straight at Shwartzie's head that knocked him on his *tuchus*. It was then that Danny and I spoke our first words to each other. *(Danny is on second base.)*

YOUNG REUVEN. Nice shot. *(Danny looks at him ... )* You always hit like that, straight at the pitcher?

DANNY. *(Matter of fact, but not pleasant.)* You're Reuven Malter.

YOUNG REUVEN. That's right.

DANNY. Your father is David Malter, the one who writes articles on Talmud?

YOUNG REUVEN. Yeah.

DANNY. *(Still flatly.)* We're going to kill you *apikorsim* this afternoon.

YOUNG REUVEN. *(Taken aback.)* Yeah, sure, rub your *tzitzit* for good luck.

REUVEN. A pleasant introduction. *(Realizing we may not quite get it. Explaining ... )* Oh. *Apikorsim.* Bad Jews. By Hasidic standards. I was an *apikoros* to Danny, despite my belief in God and Torah, because of what I read, what I thought, and what I wore — or didn't wear.

DANNY. *(Yelling, in Yiddish.)* Apikorsim, far brent zult ihr veren! ["Apikorsim, burn in hell!"]

REUVEN. The battle continued. Danny came to bat again in the third with the score tied at two a piece, one out and a man on first. *(Danny at bat. First pitch, strike. Second pitch, ball. The third he hits. Reuven jumps, grabs it, falls, flips it to shortstop, who tosses it to first, double play.)*

REUVEN/GALANTER. *(Clapping.)* Good play, Malter, good play! Okay, troops, let's go, let's go, let's go!!! *(Music plays. It is tense, no longer fun.)*

REUVEN. At the top of the fifth — we played five innings — we led five to four. Mr. Galanter paced, nervous, but pleased; the rabbi on their bench was no longer reading; our team was optimistic; and the Hasidim were now deathly quiet. Our little Sunday afternoon game was now a full-fledged holy war.

Danny was up first at the top of the fifth when Mr. Galanter put me in to pitch. *(Reuven crosses to the pitchers mound. He and Danny face off ... )* I never wanted to strike somebody out so much in my entire life. He seemed so smugly superior, so righteous, it made me furious. *(First pitch: Danny swings savagely, misses, a strike. Second pitch, the same thing again. Danny steps out of the box, looks hard at Reuven, then slowly grins ... )* After I've forgotten everything else, I will remember the devilish grin that appeared on Danny's face at that moment. I wanted, more than anything, more than winning even, to wipe that idiot grin off of his face. As I went into my windup I thought:

YOUNG REUVEN. Here's a present from an *apikoros*. *(Reuven pitches. Slow motion. Danny hits it, Reuven throws his glove up, the ball hits him in the face, he falls. Slow motion ends. Confusion, sirens. We make a transition to the hospital. Hospital sounds. Reuven is in bed. Malter enters. He has been here and dropped off the radio, which sits by the bed. He has just been conferring with the doctor. As he enters, he coughs. He is not well, but is still vital and energetic and full of love and concern for his son.)*


## Scene 3

## Imperfect Vision


YOUNG REUVEN. *(As Malter enters. He is nervous, scared ... )* What did the doctor say, *Abba?*

MALTER. He says that you are far too literal a young man. *(Beat.)*

YOUNG REUVEN. What?

MALTER. He says that next time your coach tells you to keep your eye on the ball, you should not take him quite so literally.

YOUNG REUVEN. *Abba ...*

MALTER. *(Genuinely relieved.)* He says everything should be fine. The concussion is not so serious, and they removed the piece of glass from your eye. *(Coughs.)* They want to keep you here a few days to make sure, but everything should be perfectly fine.

YOUNG REUVEN. Thank God.

MALTER. My little baseball player.

REUVEN. I could tell this incident had not increased his love of the game.

MALTER. I worry about you. I worry all the time that you will get hit by a taxi or a trolley car and you go and get hit by a baseball. *(Coughs.)*

YOUNG REUVEN. I'm sorry, *Abba ...*

MALTER. You are very fortunate. If the glass had been the tiniest bit closer to the pupil, you could have lost your sight in that eye.

YOUNG REUVEN. My God ...

MALTER. Reb Saunders called twice last night. He is very concerned.

YOUNG REUVEN. *(Amazed.)* Reb Saunders? Danny Saunders' father?

10

MALTER. He said his son was sorry for what happened.

YOUNG REUVEN. I'll just bet he's sorry. He's sorry he didn't kill me altogether!

MALTER. I don't like you to talk that way. *(Coughs.)*

YOUNG REUVEN. I hate Danny Saunders! He's making you sick!

MALTER. Me? How is he making me sick?

YOUNG REUVEN. He hit me deliberately, and now you're getting sick worrying about me.

MALTER. Deliberately?

YOUNG REUVEN. He said he would kill us *apikorsim*. They turned the game into a holy war.

MALTER. He told you it was deliberate?

YOUNG REUVEN. Well, no, but —

MALTER. So you don't *know* it was deliberate?

YOUNG REUVEN. No.

MALTER. How can you say something like that if you're not sure? That is a terrible thing to say.

YOUNG REUVEN. It seemed deliberate.

MALTER. Things are always what they seem? Since when? *(No answer.)* Since when did this miracle take place that things are always what they *seem* to be? *(No answer.)* I don't want to hear you say that again about Reb Saunders' son. He's a — I've heard he's a fine young man.

YOUNG REUVEN. Yes, *Abba*.

MALTER. Now, I brought you something. *(Shows him the radio.)* I would bring you books, but you are not to read.

YOUNG REUVEN. Not at all?

MALTER. Not until the eye is fully healed. Don't worry, I will help you with your schoolwork. And you can listen to the radio so you should not be shut off from the world. Rome may fall any day now. Great things are happening, and a radio is a blessing.

REUVEN. Anything that brought the world closer together, my father called a blessing.

MALTER. Now, I must go. You need to rest, and I have a deadline I mustn't miss.

YOUNG REUVEN. Take care of yourself, *Abba*.

MALTER. My little DiMaggio. Rest. I will see you tomorrow. *(He*

11

*leaves. Radio plays music … )*

REUVEN.  After he left I remember that I thought, probably for the first time, about my eyes. About the miracle of sight, of color, vision. I found myself consciously *looking, seeing* the hospital room, my own hands, the sky outside. When I thought about the possibility of not being able to see, not being able to read, I felt a terror seize me and I tried hard to put it from my mind. My first night alone in a hospital was a long one. *(Night. Music. Then the music warps, twists, shifts … Reuven has a vivid nightmare about Danny, the game, the accident, etc. In some way Danny shows up in the nightmare. It should be genuinely terrifying and theatrical and totally reminiscent of the game. Reuven wakes up with a start, maybe at the moment of reliving the accident. Danny stands by his bed in real life … )*

## Scene 4

### New Vision

DANNY.  Sorry if I woke you. The nurse told me it was all right for me to wait here.

YOUNG REUVEN.  *(Overlapping. Amazed, disoriented, just waking up … )* Wha … what are…?

DANNY.  How is your eye? Is it going to be all right?

YOUNG REUVEN.  Umm … yeah … maybe. *(Still waking up, turns off radio … )* No thanks to you. You could have blinded me, you know.

DANNY.  Yes, I know.

YOUNG REUVEN.  What do you want? Did you come here to gloat?

DANNY.  No. To apologize. I'm sorry for what happened.

YOUNG REUVEN.  "Sorry"? That's all?

DANNY.  You want me to be miserable? I'm that, too.

YOUNG REUVEN.  Good! You should be!

DANNY.  I did not come here to fight with you. If you just want to fight, I'll go home.

YOUNG REUVEN.  Fine, go home. *(Danny does not move.)* Well go on, what're you waiting for, an engraved invitation?

DANNY.  I came here to *talk* to you.

YOUNG REUVEN.  Well, I don't want to listen. Get the hell out of here! Go home and feel miserable! *(Beat. Then Danny starts to leave, then stops and comes back ... )* What?!? What do you want?

DANNY.  You study Talmud?

YOUNG REUVEN.  What?

DANNY.  You study Talmud, right?

YOUNG REUVEN.  Of course.

DANNY.  Yoma. Page 87b. If someone asks you for forgiveness you are supposed to grant it. I told you I am very sorry for what happened. And I'm asking you to forgive me.

YOUNG REUVEN.  Yeah, well, that passage in Yoma says you have to ask more than once. Besides, you could have killed me. In Sanhedrin ... somewhere ... it says that if someone comes to kill you —

DANNY.  You should kill them first. Sanhedrin, page 72a. But that has to do with a thief breaking into a house.

YOUNG REUVEN.  *(Impressed despite himself.)* Yeah, well, I think it applies here.

DANNY.  No it doesn't. The Talmud is very specific.

YOUNG REUVEN.  No, Raba asks that, uh, that the reason, umm ... that the law about breaking in —

DANNY.  *(With perfect recall, amazing confidence and clarity.)* "Raba asks, What's the reason for the law of breaking in. Everyone knows that a person will protect his property. So if a thief breaks in he'll have in mind that the owner will protect his property and he'll be telling himself if the owner tries to stop me, I'll kill him. Therefore the law is, if anyone comes to kill you, kill him first." *(Explaining.)* Rav asked Rabbi Hanina thirteen times to forgive him for insulting him. Rabbi Hanina refused. Rashi explains that Rav was very hard on himself in such matters, and kept asking Rabbi Hanina. But the law is you only have to ask three times. Rabbi Hanina dreamt he saw Rav suspended from a palm tree and ...

YOUNG REUVEN.  *(Finally interrupting ... )* All right, all right, all right, that's enough.

13

DANNY. I have a photographic memory. My father says it's a gift from God. I can do it with *Ivanhoe*, too. Do you want to hear?

YOUNG REUVEN. No, that's okay. I'm impressed.

DANNY. Good. I was trying to impress you. I want to talk to you.

YOUNG REUVEN. What about?

DANNY. The baseball game. I can't stop thinking about it.

YOUNG REUVEN. Yeah, neither can I.

DANNY. If I ever don't understand something, I think about it until I understand it. But I still don't understand this.

YOUNG REUVEN. Don't understand what?

DANNY. Why I wanted to kill you.

YOUNG REUVEN. *(Utterly amazed.)* What???

DANNY. I don't understand why I wanted to kill you. *(Beat.)* It's really bothering me.

YOUNG REUVEN. Well, I should hope so.

DANNY. Don't be cute, Malter. I really wanted to kill you.

YOUNG REUVEN. Why?

DANNY. I don't know. That's what I'm telling you. But I did. Remember right before that last pitch you threw me, I smiled at you?

YOUNG REUVEN. I remember. Believe me.

DANNY. It was right then. At that moment it just hit me. I wanted to step over the plate and ... and just open your head up with the baseball bat.

YOUNG REUVEN. *(Amazed again.)* Wha...?

DANNY. And it wasn't your whole team or anything, just you. Like it was just you and me out there, and I just ... I just wanted to — I don't know, to — get you.

YOUNG REUVEN. Well, it was a pretty hot game. And I wasn't exactly wild about you, either.

DANNY. I don't think you even know what I'm talking about.

YOUNG REUVEN. Now wait a minute —

DANNY. It wasn't the game. It was *you*. You really had me going there, Malter.

YOUNG REUVEN. Quit calling me Malter. You sound like a teacher or something.

DANNY. So what should I call you?

YOUNG REUVEN. If you have to call me anything, call me Reuven.

14

DANNY.  Okay. And call me Danny.

YOUNG REUVEN.  Okay.

REUVEN.  It was surreal. I'd never heard a Hasid speak anything but Yiddish before, yet here was Danny Saunders, whom I thought I hated, dressed as a Hasid, speaking perfect English, chatting about how he wanted to kill me because of some curve-balls I'd thrown him.

DANNY.  You know, you're a pretty rough player.

YOUNG REUVEN.  So are you. Why do you always hit like that?

DANNY.  Like what?

YOUNG REUVEN.  Straight back at the pitcher.

DANNY.  I don't know. I don't try. It just happens that way. Maybe the way I hold the bat. But I've never hurt anyone before. You were supposed to duck.

YOUNG REUVEN.  I had no chance to duck.

DANNY.  Sure you did.

YOUNG REUVEN.  There wasn't enough time.

DANNY.  There was time for you to bring up your glove.

YOUNG REUVEN.  Yeah, but … *(He is caught, considering this for the first time … )* Huh …

DANNY.  *(Putting it together for the first time … )* Maybe you did-n't want to duck.

YOUNG REUVEN.  *(Realizing along with him.)* Maybe I didn't.

DANNY.  *(Still putting it together a piece at a time.)* Maybe you did-n't want to because I was the one who hit it. Maybe you didn't want to duck any ball that I hit.

YOUNG REUVEN.  Right …

DANNY.  You had to stop it.

YOUNG REUVEN.  I think that's right.

DANNY.  Like I wanted to "stop" you.

YOUNG REUVEN.  Yeah, I guess so.

DANNY.  Well, you stopped it.

YOUNG REUVEN.  Yeah. I stopped it all right. *(Beat.)*

DANNY.  I better get going. I have school.

YOUNG REUVEN.  Oh, by the way, who won the game?

DANNY.  Oh. We did. Sorry.

YOUNG REUVEN.  Maybe you should be a professional baseball player.

DANNY. I don't think my father would be too happy about that.

YOUNG REUVEN. He'd say it was a game for *goyim*, huh?

DANNY. I don't know what he would say. He doesn't talk to me very much.

YOUNG REUVEN. Come on. He's a rabbi and he doesn't talk much?

DANNY. Oh, he talks a lot, just not to me.

YOUNG REUVEN. I don't understand.

DANNY. He prefers silence. He once told me he wished that we all could talk in silence.

YOUNG REUVEN. Talk in silence?

DANNY. That's what he said.

YOUNG REUVEN. I don't get it.

DANNY. I don't either. *(Beat.)* I better go.

YOUNG REUVEN. Okay.

DANNY. I'll come again tomorrow … if it's okay with you.

YOUNG REUVEN. Sure. *(Danny starts out as Malter approaches from the other side.)* Danny?

DANNY. Yes?

YOUNG REUVEN. Thanks for coming.

DANNY. Thanks for listening.


## Scene 5

## A Friend


*The scene instantly shifts and Malter is with his son. Danny leaves, or perhaps remains on stage, elsewhere …*


YOUNG REUVEN. Danny Saunders came to see me today.

MALTER. Ah. And?

YOUNG REUVEN. I … I like him.

MALTER. So? You like him? And what has caused this miracle?

REUVEN. I told him of our whole conversation.

MALTER. People are not always what they seem to be. That is the way the world is.

YOUNG REUVEN. He's so different from what I thought he'd be.

MALTER. The Talmud says that a person should do two things for himself. One is to acquire a teacher. Do you remember the other?

YOUNG REUVEN. Choose a friend.

MALTER. Very good. You know what a friend is? A Greek philosopher said that true friends are like two bodies with one soul. Reuven, listen to me now. If you can, I think you should make Danny Saunders your friend, and let him make you his friend.

YOUNG REUVEN. I like him a lot, *Abba.*

MALTER. I am not talking about liking only. I am talking about true friendship, about ... *(Coughs.)*

DANNY. *(Entering or stepping forward from where he has been outside the scene.)* It's like suddenly seeing whole new worlds just open up in front of me.

YOUNG REUVEN. I understand.

MALTER. Make him your friend. I think I am right in this. *(He coughs again ... )*

DANNY. *(Approaching the scene.)* Worlds that I had no idea existed until just a few months ago.

YOUNG REUVEN. How are you, *Abba?*

MALTER. I am tired, Reuven. Just a little tired. *(Malter exits; the scene cross-fades. Next day.)*

DANNY. *(Entering the scene.)* Have you read Hemingway?

YOUNG REUVEN. Some.

DANNY. And Tolstoy?

YOUNG REUVEN. No.

DANNY. What about Dostoyevsky? Have you read *The Brothers Karamazov?*

YOUNG REUVEN. Yes. Have you???

DANNY. Isn't it amazing? I met this man at the library and I asked him for suggestions. He gave it to me.

YOUNG REUVEN. You've been asking strangers for books?

DANNY. He's been very helpful. I didn't know where to start. I'd never been to a public library before.

YOUNG REUVEN. Right ...

DANNY. I just get so tired of studying Talmud all the time. I know the stuff cold, it gets boring. So I've been spending almost every afternoon at the library.

YOUNG REUVEN. Aren't secular books forbidden?

DANNY. Yes, of course. Last month I started reading Freud. Do you know much about Freud?

YOUNG REUVEN. No, not much.

DANNY. It's all about what we're really like, deep down inside, in what he calls "the unconscious." He says the most mysterious thing in the universe is man himself. We're blind about the thing we are closest to. Isn't that fascinating?

YOUNG REUVEN. Yeah.

DANNY. Freud writes a lot about dreams. Our dreams are tied to our unconscious. You can learn all sorts of things about yourself if you understand your dreams. Did you know that? That's what Freud started. He gives us a new way of looking at the world ... and ourselves. *(Beat.)* My father once told me that a Jew's only mission in life is to obey God. But sometimes I'm just not sure what God wants.

REUVEN. My father always told me you can't judge a book by its cover. But this book and its cover seemed to come from entirely different planets ...

YOUNG REUVEN. You know, you look like a Hasid, but you sure don't sound like one.

DANNY. How is a Hasid supposed to sound?

YOUNG REUVEN. Not like you. Freud? Hemingway? And it sounds like you don't believe in God.

DANNY. I believe in God! I never said I don't believe in God.

YOUNG REUVEN. Are you really going to be a rabbi?

DANNY. Of course. I'll be *tzaddik* after my father. My family has led our people for six generations.

YOUNG REUVEN. Wow.

DANNY. So what do I sound like?

YOUNG REUVEN. What?

DANNY. If I don't sound like a Hasid, what do I sound like?

YOUNG REUVEN. Like... like an *apikoros*. *(Beat. Reuven hears his father ... )* Wait. Here comes my father. I'm glad you can meet him. *(As Malter arrives, he and Danny stare at each other ... )*

YOUNG REUVEN. *Abba*, this is Danny Saunders. Danny, this

18

is my father.

MALTER. Hello, Daniel. I understand you play baseball as fiercely as you read.

DANNY. *(Utterly amazed.)* You're David Malter? I had no idea.

YOUNG REUVEN. What's going...?

MALTER. How could you. We only talked literature. I never told you my name.

YOUNG REUVEN. *(Putting it together.)* Wait a second! You're the man from the library? You gave him *Hemingway?!?*

MALTER. Ah, I see Daniel has already confided in you his reading habits.

YOUNG REUVEN. Why didn't you tell me?

MALTER. I didn't think it was for me to tell.

YOUNG REUVEN. Even after the accident? I've been —

MALTER. I meet a young boy in the library while I'm doing research. A Hasid. He sits in a back corner where he can't be seen. We nod, smile. We see each other for several days. Eventually he asks me for a recommendation, "anything that is worthwhile." I suggest a book. Two hours later he comes back and he has not only read it and understood it, it seems he has memorized it. We discuss it a little. I recommend another. The same thing happens. All I understand is that here is a hungry mind and I do my best to nourish it with "worthwhile" food. Then I find out from the librarian he is Danny Saunders, Reb Saunders' son, so now I understand the need for secrecy. I did not think it was for me to tell. You understand?

DANNY. I'm very grateful to you, Mr. Malter.

MALTER. No need. Soon you will not need anyone to make recommendations. And have you started on Freud yet, as you said?

DANNY. A little. I am trying to learn German first so I can read him in the original.

MALTER. Ah, I see. Of course.

DANNY. I better go. I'll come over on *Shabbos.* Is that all right?

YOUNG REUVEN. Yeah, good.

DANNY. Good-bye, Mr. Malter.

MALTER. Good-bye, Daniel. *(To Reuven.)* Come, my little baseball player. We are going home.

# Scene 6

## A New World

*Music. Transition. During this section Reuven wanders through his old home again in his memory.*

REUVEN. As I rode home from the hospital with my father that June afternoon, and I put on my spare glasses, the world suddenly seemed to leap into focus. Everything looked fresh and clean and new. And as I walked through our house I felt as though I were actually *seeing* it for the first time. The worn gray carpet and the pictures of Herzl and Chaim Weizmann in the entrance hall; the smell of chicken soup coming from the kitchen; my bed; my desk; my books; the war maps; and the pictures of President Roosevelt and Albert Einstein that I had cut out of *Senior Scholastic* and pasted on my walls; even the ailanthus tree just outside my window, everything ... Everything seemed sharpened, and pulsing with life. I remember feeling that I had somehow crossed into another world, as if a little piece of my old self lay shattered in the school yard along with my glasses. *(Beat. Young Reuven enters from one side, dressed in a jacket, Danny from another, and they meet up and begin walking together. During the scene they walk to Danny's house ... )* Danny came over the next afternoon as he had promised.

DANNY. I thought we'd go over to my father's shul. He wants to meet you.

YOUNG REUVEN. Where is it?

DANNY. On Sharon Avenue, just off of Lee.

REUVEN. Only five blocks. Five blocks and a world away.

YOUNG REUVEN. Is this all right? I don't have a caftan, you know.

DANNY. A jacket is fine. Caftans are only required for members of the fold.

YOUNG REUVEN. Okay, member of the fold, so why does your

father want to meet me?

DANNY. I told him we're friends, so he wants to meet you. Is that okay?

YOUNG REUVEN. Sure, I'm happy to meet him.

DANNY. No, I mean, that I told him we're friends.

YOUNG REUVEN. Oh. Yeah, that's fine, that's good.

DANNY. He has to approve of my friends, especially if they're outside the fold.

YOUNG REUVEN. Wow! *(Music plays.)*

REUVEN. As we walked, I wondered what my classmates would think if they saw me with Danny. It seemed somehow ... odd to be with him. As if the world had tipped slightly ...

YOUNG REUVEN. So, your father wants to find out why you'd be friends with an *apikoros*, huh?

DANNY. I guess. He just said, "I'll meet him." I was surprised he said that much.

YOUNG REUVEN. Right ... You said he doesn't talk to you. But you don't mean ... never, right?

DANNY. Hardly ever. "I'll meet him" was a long conversation.

YOUNG REUVEN. Does he talk to your mother?

DANNY. Sure.

YOUNG REUVEN. And your little brother?

DANNY. Yes. Him, too.

YOUNG REUVEN. But not you?

DANNY. No.

YOUNG REUVEN. I'd hate that.

DANNY. It isn't pleasant, but he's a great man, and I'm sure he has his reasons.

YOUNG REUVEN. Well, my father's a great man, too, but —

DANNY. You have no idea of the life he's led. He has had to be *tzaddik* since he was only a little older than we are. This was in Russia, before the Great War. And he was married back then, too, and had a son, and already more than a thousand followers. Then, when he was only about twenty-five their village was raided by Cossacks. They burnt the synagogue and hundreds and hundreds of his followers were killed. His wife and son were killed. He was shot in the chest and left for dead.

YOUNG REUVEN. Oh my God ...

21

DANNY. When he recovered he gathered his followers, almost three-hundred people in all, and brought them out of Russia through Austria and France and England to America. It took them more than six months. But they got here, and because of him they were able to start a new life.

YOUNG REUVEN. And they all just followed him? Just like that?

DANNY. Sure. They would follow him anywhere. He's not just a rabbi, he's a *tzaddik*.

YOUNG REUVEN. I thought a *tzaddik* was a rabbi.

DANNY. No, he's more of ... of a messenger. The *tzaddik* is like a bridge between the people and God. They look to him for spiritual guidance and leadership — where to live, what job to do, who to marry, everything.

YOUNG REUVEN. And that'll be you someday?

DANNY. That's the idea.

YOUNG REUVEN. And they just do what he tells them?

DANNY. Sure. They respect him. They feel that ... he knows what's best for them.

YOUNG REUVEN. Wow. I don't understand how anyone can follow someone so blindly. It sounds more like the Pope — like a king or something.

DANNY. Well, that's the way it is, whether you understand it or not. Here. You can see for yourself.

YOUNG REUVEN. *(A little apprehensive.)* Great. *(We hear voices, men and boys, all speaking Yiddish, gathering at Saunders' shul ...)*

REUVEN. On the street outside the shul, the flock had begun to assemble. As we approached, as they saw Danny, the crowds just parted to let him through. *(We see and hear this. Throughout this scene we hear the appropriate sounds of the shul, as in a movie. It is ominous and intimidating ... )*

YOUNG REUVEN. *(Whisper.)* I feel like a cowboy surrounded by Indians.

DANNY. *(Whisper.)* You're in the holy halls now. It takes some getting used to.

YOUNG REUVEN. *(Whisper.)* It was like the parting of the Red Sea out there. How'd you do it?

DANNY. *(Whisper.)* I'm my father's son, remember, the inheritor of the dynasty. *(The room quiets.)* Shhh ... My father is coming. *(Dead silence. Saunders approaches. We hear his footsteps echo through the hallowed halls. His approach is terrifying and awesome ... )*

REUVEN.  As he passed each row of seats, men rose, bowed slightly, and sat again. Some reached out to touch him. He walked slowly and deliberately and with enormous dignity. I had never seen anyone get that kind of response before. The congregation at our shul respected our rabbi and even loved him, but this was totally different. This was ... awe.

DANNY.  *(Who has stood as his father approached.)* Tatte. This is Reuven Malter.

REUVEN.  I could feel every eye in the place boring into me.

SAUNDERS.  You are the son of David Malter?

YOUNG REUVEN.  Yes.

SAUNDERS.  Your eye. It is healed?

YOUNG REUVEN.  It's going to be fine, thank you.

SAUNDERS.  You know mathematics? My son tells me you are very good in mathematics.

YOUNG REUVEN.  Yes ...

SAUNDERS.  We will see. And you know Hebrew. A son of David Malter surely knows Hebrew?

YOUNG REUVEN.  Yes.

SAUNDERS.  We will see.

REUVEN.  And with that Reb Saunders took his place and the service began.*(Service begins ... )* It was not so different from the one in the shul I had attended with my father only that morning. The familiarity of the prayers in this strange new land was, as my father would have said, a blessing. *(The service is over. Saunders prepares to speak.)* When the service was over, there was silence. A long, solid silence, as every eye and ear in the shul focused entirely on Reb Saunders. No one moved, or spoke, or even seemed to breathe. I felt Danny go absolutely still and tense in front of me, almost like a soldier poised for combat. Finally, Reb Saunders began to speak. His followers hung on every word.

SAUNDERS.  Rabbi Halafta son of Dosa teaches us, "When ten people sit together and occupy themselves with Torah, the Presence of God abides among them." Torah gives us strength! Torah clothes us! Torah brings the Presence! But to study Torah is a task for all day and all night. Does not Rabbi Meir teach us, "He who is walking by the way and studying, and breaks off his study and says "How fine is that tree, how fine is that field," him the scripture regards as if he had forfeited his life"? His life! So great is the study of Torah. Now listen: Whose task is it to study Torah? The world? No! What does the world know of Torah? The world is *Esav!* The world is *Amalek!* The world is Cossacks! The world is Hitler, may his name and memory be erased! Of whom, then? Of the people of Israel! *We* are to study His Torah! *We* are commanded to sit in the light of the Presence! It is written, "This world is like a vestibule before the world-to-come; prepare thyself in the vestibule, that thou mayest enter the hall." In *gematriya*, the words "this world" add up to 163, and the words "world-to-come" come out to 154. The difference between "this world" and "the world-to-come" is nine. Nine is half of eighteen. Eighteen is *chai*, life. In this world, there is only half of *chai*. We are only half alive in this world. Only half alive!

REUVEN. This was *gematriya*, an ancient form of numerology. In Hebrew each letter is also a number so every word also has a numeric value. These numbers could be manipulated as Reb Saunders was now doing.

SAUNDERS. How can we make our lives full so that we are eighteen, *chai*, and not half *chai*? Rabbi Joshua son of Levi teaches us, "Whoever does not labor in the Torah is said to be under the divine censure." He is a *nozuf*, hated by the Master of the Universe. A righteous man, a *tzaddik*, studies Torah. In *gematriya*, *nozuf* is 143, and *tzaddik* is 204. What is the difference between *nozuf* and *tzaddik*? Sixty-one. To whom does a *tzaddik* dedicate his life? To God, to *La-el!* The word, *La-el* in *gematriya* is sixty-one. It is a life dedicated to God that makes the difference between *nozuf* and *tzaddik!*

In *gematriya*, the letter of the word *traklin*, hall, the hall that refers to the world-to-come is 399, and *prozdor*, the vestibule that is this world, comes out 513. Take *traklin* from *prozdor* and we have 114. Now listen to me. A righteous man, a *tzaddik*, we said, comes out to 204. A righteous man lives by Torah. Torah is *mayim*, water; the great and holy rabbis always compare Torah to water. The word *mayim* in *gematriya* is ninety. Take *mayim* from *tzaddik* and we also have 114! From this we learn that the righteous man who removes himself from Torah also removes himself from the world-to-come! Without Torah there is only half a life. When we study Torah, then the Master of the Universe listens. Then he hears our words. May Torah be a fountain of waters to all who drink from it, and may it bring to us the Messiah speedily and in our day, Amen! *(In a different tone:)* Nu, Daniel, you have anything to say? *(Danny nods "yes.")* Nu, what is it?

DANNY. *(Standing, or going to his father. To the congregation:)* It is written in the name of Rabbi Yaakov. About breaking off from studying Torah, it is written in the name of Rabbi Yaakov, not Rabbi Meir.

SAUNDERS. Yes. Good. It is written in the name of Rabbi Yaakov. And nothing more? *(Danny shakes his head "no," surprised by the question.)* No? Nothing more?

DANNY. No.

SAUNDERS. Absolutely nothing more to say?

DANNY. I didn't hear —

SAUNDERS. You did not hear! You did not hear. You heard the first mistake, and you stopped listening. How could you hear when you were not listening? *(Danny is frozen, puzzling ... And then he begins to grin, as he begins to understand, the same grin from when he looked at Reuven at the baseball game ... )* So. You have nothing more to say. Perhaps I am wrong to expect it. After all my son is not a mathematician. But we have a mathematician with us. The son of David Malter is with us, and he is a mathematician. Reuven ... *(He beckons him up front. Reuven stands or goes to him.)* You have nothing to say?

YOUNG REUVEN. *(On the spot. Shaking his head "no," quietly ...)* Uh-uh.

SAUNDERS. You heard my little talk? *(Reuven nods "yes.")* And you have nothing to say? *(Reuven nods "no.")* You liked the *gematriya*?

YOUNG REUVEN. *(Quietly, tentatively.)* Yes.

SAUNDERS. Good. I am very happy. Which *gematriya* did you like?

YOUNG REUVEN. They were all very good.

SAUNDERS. All? A very nice compliment. But were they? Were they all very good? *(Reuven is unsure, confused ... )* Were *all* the *gematryios* good, Reuven?

YOUNG REUVEN. *(Barely audible.)* No.

SAUNDERS. Oh?

YOUNG REUVEN. *(A tiny bit stronger.)* No, they were not all good.

SAUNDERS. *Nu*, Reuven, tell us which one was not good.

YOUNG REUVEN. The *gematriya* for *prozdor* is 503, not 513.

SAUNDERS. *(Neutral.)* The *gematriya* for *prozdor* comes out 503. *(Big smile.)* Good. Very good. *(There is a murmur of approval from the crowd. Music starts, the service is over, we hear the sounds of the congregation. Danny and Reuven rush away form the crowd.)*

YOUNG REUVEN. What the hell was *that* all about?

DANNY. I'm sorry. I had no idea he would —

YOUNG REUVEN. What was that, some kind of test?

DANNY. Sort of. That was very good the way you caught that —

YOUNG REUVEN. Does he do that every week?

DANNY. Sure. I don't mind it. It's a family tradition. It's kind of a game, almost.

YOUNG REUVEN. Some game! In front of everyone.

DANNY. They love it. They're proud to see us like that.

SAUNDERS. *(Approaching.)* Reuven. You have a good head on you. I know of your father. I am not surprised you have such a head. Your father is a great scholar. But what he writes, ah, what he writes ... But your father is an observer of the commandments, yes?

YOUNG REUVEN. Yes, yes of course.

SAUNDERS. Then it is good you are my Daniel's friend. It is good. I have many responsibilities. I ... I am not always able to talk to him. You think a friend is an easy thing to be? If you are truly his friend, you will discover otherwise. *(Malter enters and goes to his study.)* *Nu*, it is late and your father will be worried. Come and pray with us again. There will be no more mistakes in *gematriya*. *(Music plays. It is late at night. Quiet. Peaceful. Both sons take tea in to their fathers.)*

REUVEN. When I got home I made some tea for myself and my father and I told him everything. I always looked forward enormously to these latenight talks with my father. They let me sort things out in my own head as well as gain his perspective. He always listened carefully and never treated anything I said as foolish ...

MALTER. Well, you had some day, Reuven.

REUVEN. Although I'm sure I often was.

YOUNG REUVEN. It was an experience, *Abba. (Add Danny and Saunders.)*

DANNY. *(In Yiddish.) Tatte. Wilst un glassele tea? (Saunders nods and motions where to put it down. Danny pours him tea and some for himself and sits. Long pause. Silence ... Shift to Reuven and Malter.)*

YOUNG REUVEN. Reb Saunders is confusing. His followers seem in awe of him. And he seems cruel and distant at one moment, and then suddenly he is kind and almost ... tender.

MALTER. Reb Saunders is a great man, Reuven, and great men are always difficult to understand. He carries the burden of many people on his shoulders. I do not care for his Hasidism very much, but it is not a simple task to be a leader of people. And he is not a fraud. He could make a great contribution, but he occupies himself only with Talmud. And Danny will do the same when he takes his place. What a waste. It is a shame that a mind like Danny's will be shut off from the rest of the world. *(Shift to Danny and Saunders.)*

DANNY. *(In Yiddish.) Ich bin zayer su frieden, tatte, az hir hut mein frient bekant. ["I am glad you met my friend, Father."] (Saunders looks at Danny, nods, reads. Long pause. Silence ... Shift to Reuven and Malter.)*

YOUNG REUVEN. I thought it was terrible the way he made Danny try to catch his mistakes.

MALTER. It is not terrible, not for Danny and not for the people who listened. It is an old tradition. And it is not only among rabbis. The same thing happens in a university. When you become a professor, you will have to defend your ideas. If you have a contribution to make, you must make it in public. *(Shift to Danny and Saunders. The silence continues ... Shift to Reuven and Malter.)*

YOUNG REUVEN. Danny told me that he'll also be going to Hirsch College in the fall.

MALTER. *(Surprised.)* Not a Hasidic yeshiva?

YOUNG REUVEN. His father wants him to study Talmud with Rav Gershenson. So I guess you and Reb Saunders have at least one thing in common.

MALTER. Oh? What's that?

YOUNG REUVEN. You want nothing but the best teachers in the world for your sons. *(Shift to Danny and Saunders. The silence*

*continues ... Add Reuven and Malter.)*
YOUNG REUVEN. I have some reading to do for school. Will we study together tomorrow?
MALTER. Yes, in the afternoon. I have a deadline. *(Reuven and Danny both start to go, clearing the tea away, getting ready to go to bed ... )* I'm very proud of the way you handled yourself today. I am glad Reb Saunders will let you and Danny be friends.
YOUNG REUVEN. Me, too.
DANNY. *Gut nacht, tatte. (Saunders nods good night without looking up ... )*
YOUNG REUVEN. Good night, *Abba.*
MALTER. Good night, Reuven. Pleasant dreams.
SAUNDERS. *(After Danny and Reuven are gone. In Yiddish. To himself ... ) Gut nacht, mine Daniel. Gut nacht ...*

# Scene 7

## The Silence

*Music plays. With energy and enthusiasm, breaking the previous mood.*

REUVEN. My final year of yeshiva was hectic. I was class president, homework filled my spare time, and I studied Talmud both at school, and at home on the weekends. I had other friends, and we'd go to parties sometimes, or the movies (an activity Reb Saunders forbade) but most of my time I spent with Danny.

We would go on walks or to the library where we would read, do our schoolwork, talk, or sometimes just sit quietly ... I avoided going back to Reb Saunders' shul, even though Danny told me his father had asked him repeatedly when I was coming to study with them. Finally, in early November, we agreed that on the following Shabbat I would come over in the afternoon. *(The boys have arrived in Saunders' study.)*

SAUNDERS. So, you are a good mathematician. Now we will see what you know about more important things. We will start, yes?

REUVEN. And it began!

SAUNDERS. *(Jumping ahead, right into the thick of it, as though it has been going on for some time already. This is impassioned and intense, a battle, an enjoyable battle, with ideas and references for weapons ...)* The wives are childless when their husband dies.

DANNY. That's in tractate Yevamot, the first Mishnah.

SAUNDERS. Yes, good. *(To Reuven.)* And in the Torah?

YOUNG REUVEN. Devorim. Chapter ... twenty-five?

SAUNDERS. Good. Go on.

YOUNG REUVEN. *(Remembering.)* If a man dies childless, his widow is obligated to marry his brother, in order for the dead brother to have an heir.

SAUNDERS. Good! *(The rest of the Talmud battle scene continues silently, or at a barely audible whisper, under this narration. If it is done aggressively, it should time out right.)*

REUVEN. But it was less of a discussion than a pitched battle. They argued fiercely, quoting from tractates all through the Talmud, grabbing texts to support their views, arguing so fiercely I thought they might even come to blows at one point. But there was a kind of ... intimacy in their arguing that I found astonishing. They both clearly took great joy in the battle, and if Reb Saunders looked pleased when he won, he looked even more pleased when Danny won. Soon my nervousness disappeared and I eagerly joined the fray. *(He listens to pick up the thread of the argument. When he has, he speaks again:)*

SAUNDERS. *(Starting after "Good!" Silently.)* And what is the difficulty in such a case?

DANNY. *(Silently.)* One of the two wives is the daughter of the living brother.

SAUNDERS. *(Silently.)* Meaning?

YOUNG REUVEN. *(Silently.)* The dead brother had married his own niece.

SAUNDERS. *(Silently.)* Yes, obviously. And what does that mean?

DANNY. *(Silently.)* If the living brother marries her, he'll be marrying his own daughter.

YOUNG REUVEN. *(Silently.)* But he can't marry her. The Torah forbids it. That would be incest.

SAUNDERS. *(Silently.)* Of course he cannot marry her. But what about the second wife?

YOUNG REUVEN. *(Silently.)* He can't marry her either, according to the first Mishnah.

SAUNDERS. *(Silently.)* He can't marry her either. Everyone holds that way?

DANNY. *(Silently.)* The school of Hillel holds that way. But the school of Shammai holds that the other wife is permitted to marry her dead husband's brother.

SAUNDERS. *(Silently.)* Yes, the school of Shammai says the other wife is permitted to marry ... And? What is the difficulty with this?

DANNY. *(Out loud.)* According to the School of Hillel, because the other wife was forbidden to the living brother, if they have a child, the child is a *momzer.*

SAUNDERS. *(Out loud.)* A *momzer,* yes.

REUVEN. In the Talmud a dispute is recorded between two well-known schools of rabbis, the schools of Hillel and Shammai, over the case of two women married to the same man ...

YOUNG REUVEN. *(Silently.)* The child is unfit to marry a fit Jew.

SAUNDERS. *(Silently.)* And according to the school of Shammai?

DANNY. *(Silently.)* The child is a fit Jew and is permitted to marry a fit Jew.

SAUNDERS. *(Silently.)* Yes. The child is a fit Jew. And how does the Mishnah end, Reuven?

DANNY. *(Out loud from here on.)* The school of Shammai did not refrain from marrying women of the school of Hillel, nor did the school of Hillel refrain from marrying women of the school of Shammai."

SAUNDERS. Good.

YOUNG REUVEN. I remember now. There's more!

SAUNDERS. Yes?

YOUNG REUVEN. The Mishnah also says that even though they differed on matters of ritual purity, the women still lent each other their pots and pans, prepared food together, and ate in each other's homes.

SAUNDERS. *(Dubious.)* Yes, the Mishnah says that. But now I ask you, Reuven: Could such a thing be possible?

YOUNG REUVEN. The Mishnah says yes.

SAUNDERS. *(Putting him on the spot.)* I do not understand how such a thing could be possible ... *(Beat.)*

YOUNG REUVEN. Maybe they didn't ask each other too many questions.

DANNY. Later in the Talmud it says that the School of Shammai never put into practice what it taught in this case of the childless dead husband.

YOUNG REUVEN. Who said that?

DANNY. Rav said it? *(Saunders nods.)*

YOUNG REUVEN. How did Rav know?

DANNY. What do you mean?

YOUNG REUVEN. He lived hundreds of years after Hillel and Shammai.

DANNY. Rav was a great sage.

YOUNG REUVEN. But he lived in Babylonia, not Palestine, where Hillel and Shammai lived. My father once told me that when one of the sages says something described in the Torah or the Talmud never really happened, it only means he doesn't understand it.

SAUNDERS. *(Sharply.)* You question the greatness of Rav?

DANNY. In the Jerusalem Talmud it says God made sure nothing wrong ever happened in such a marriage.

YOUNG REUVEN. Then it becomes God's job. My father told me that the Jerusalem Talmud says "both sides in this dispute speak in God's voice." I think it's great that both schools respected each other's views.

SAUNDERS. Perhaps. But there are limits to such respect. *(A sudden break.)* Now, Daniel, perhaps you would be good enough to bring us some tea. *(Danny is hesitant ... )*

YOUNG REUVEN. I'm fine, Reb Saunders.

SAUNDERS. Daniel, please. *(Danny goes. As he leaves ... )* Reuven, please turn to the end of the chapter. Page forty. You see where it says "Better a man should sin in secret"? You see it. Read.

YOUNG REUVEN. *(He is unsure, but begins to read ... )* "Better a man should sin in secret than profane God's name publicly, for it is said to sin is to lose one's future life — "

SAUNDERS. Good. Enough. *(Reuven stops, confused ... )* So. You have a good head. Now we will see about your soul. Reuven, I know my Daniel spends hours most days in the library. No, do not say anything. You are surprised I know. This neighborhood is not so big ... He does not come home in the afternoons week after week, I want to know where he is. So, now I know. I also know he is sometimes there with you, sometimes with your father. Reuven: I want to know what he reads. I want you to tell me.

YOUNG REUVEN. *(An impossible situation.)* I ... I don't know what to say.

SAUNDERS. You are being loyal, and that is good in a friend. But please, hear me out. I will not live forever. Daniel must one day take my place. My son is my most precious possession. I must know what he is reading and I cannot ask him. So I am asking you. Please. *(Beat.)* Please ...

REUVEN. *(Unsure, haltingly ... )* He reads a lot ... He is very curious about the world. Dostoyevsky ... Hemingway ... A little Darwin. Freud. He is very interested in the human mind, in psychology.

SAUNDERS. *(Mostly to God and himself.)* Psychology? Master of the Universe, psychology ... What can I do? What can I do? The pain of raising children. So many troubles ... Reuven, you and your father, you will be a good influence on my son, yes? You will not make a *goy* out of my son?

REUVEN. I was amazed at the bewildered pain, the ache in his voice. *(Danny returns with tea.)*

SAUNDERS. So ... so, Reuven, tell me more of your father's method of study. Correcting the texts, eh? You ... eh, you believe that this is right?

YOUNG REUVEN. I ... yes, yes, I think so, in cases where the ... uh, where the text and the, uh ...

DANNY. What just happened? *(To his father.)* What happened while I was gone? What did you say to him? *(Saunders says nothing.)*

YOUNG REUVEN. Danny, it's okay.

DANNY. What happened? *(Saunders says nothing.)* Why won't...? *(He walks quickly out. Beat.)*

SAUNDERS. Reuven, I am sorry.

YOUNG REUVEN. It's ... I ... I'm going to find Danny.

*(Reuven runs outside to where Danny is, very upset, confused, angry ... )* He knows. He asked about the library, about what you are reading. And I told him. I figured he would find out one way or another. And I couldn't lie to him. I'm sorry ...

DANNY. *(Quiet. Intense. This scene begins with great restraint.)* I just wish he had asked *me.*

YOUNG REUVEN. Why didn't he?

DANNY. I told you! He believes in silence. When I was ten or eleven I complained to him about something and he told me to close my mouth and to look into my soul. He told me to stop running to him every time I have a problem. I should look into my own soul for the answer. So now we just ... don't ... talk.

YOUNG REUVEN. What happens if you try?

DANNY. I can't now! Maybe it sounds crazy to you, but it's true.

YOUNG REUVEN. I think you ought to at least try.

DANNY. *(Exploding.)* I *can't!* Don't you understand English? I *can't talk to him!!!* I'm sorry if you don't understand, I can't explain it any better than I have. *(Danny leaves.)*

YOUNG REUVEN. I'm sorry, I — *(He gets up to follow, and then lets Danny go. Jump-cut to the Malter home ... )*

MALTER. Silence? What do you mean Danny is being brought up in silence?

YOUNG REUVEN. They never talk except when they study Talmud. That's what Danny told me.

MALTER. Ah, dear God ...

YOUNG REUVEN. What is it?

MALTER. Once I heard something about this, but I did not believe it ...

YOUNG REUVEN. Heard what, *Abba?*

MALTER. I cannot explain. I cannot explain what I do not understand. *(Beat.)* I am happy Reb Saunders knows about his son's reading. I was concerned about all the subterfuge. I do not often agree with him, but I respect him. He is a great leader.

YOUNG REUVEN. But why can't he talk to Danny?

MALTER. He has talked to Danny. He has talked to Danny through you. *(Beat.)* It is never pleasant to be a buffer, Reuven. And it is not always such an easy thing to be a true friend, is it...?

# Scene 8

## The News

*Radio news. Both fathers and sons listen together. Music under this whole section. We see the reaction of both families to the news as it unfolds.*

REUVEN. The war continued in Europe. The Allied armies were advancing, and by the spring rumors began to spread that the war would soon be over. Then in mid-April, like a thunderclap, came the news of President Roosevelt's death. No one could believe it. I had never thought of him as mortal, and it seemed absurd and impossible for him to die, especially with the end of the war so close and his new United Nations ready to meet.

On the day he died I remember riding home on the trolley in complete silence. I sat next to a tiny old man in a dark brown suit with a wilted flower in his buttonhole. He held thick glasses in one hand and wept openly the entire trip. I'll never forget him and the sense of loss, irreparable loss we all felt that day. My father and I now listened to the radio at every meal, something we had never done. *(Radio news plays news of Hitler's death. Both families hear it and react ... )* Finally, at the beginning of May came the news of the end of the war. And with this news of great rejoicing, the news of Hitler's concentration camps and the mounting death toll of one million ... three million ... four million ... as many as six million Jews exterminated throughout Europe.

SAUNDERS. *(Almost numb, sad and pained beyond belief. Reuven and Danny sit in his study, listening ... )* The world kills us. Ah, how the world kills us. In the past it destroyed a village of Jews here, a city of Jews there ... Now — everything, everyone — all of Europe ... gone ... *(Beat.)* What a Jewish world that was. Synagogues, schools, homes, markets, books. Even the muddy roads I walked on to my father's shul, even these roads seemed

somehow sacred ... And they would freeze in the winter, and I would slide on them, and sliding would bring me quicker to my school than if I'd walked. My friends and I, playing and sliding on those roads under the frozen trees ... The Sabbaths, the festivals, the singing and dancing, the study of Torah, the people, all the people — all gone into heaps of bones and ashes. *(A cry.)* Master of the Universe, how do you permit such a thing to happen? *(Long pause. Regaining his composure.)* But it is the will of God. It is the will of God, and we must accept God's will. *(Move back to Malter's. Reuven is now with his father while Danny remains with his.)*

MALTER. *(Picking up in the middle of the conversation.)* "God's will"? Reb Saunders said it is "God's will"? *(Reuven nods.)* And are you satisfied with that answer?

YOUNG REUVEN. *(Quietly.)* No.

MALTER. No. No. Good. I am not satisfied with it, either.

YOUNG REUVEN. He kept asking, How can God let such a thing happen?

MALTER. And did God answer him? Did God answer him, Reuven? *(No answer.)* We cannot wait for God. If there is an answer we must make it ourselves. Six million have been slaughtered. It will have meaning only if we *give* it meaning. We cannot wait for God. There is only one Jewry left now in the world. It is here, in America. We have a terrible responsibility. We will need teachers and rabbis now to lead our people. The Jewish world is changed forever. A madman has destroyed our treasures. If we do not rebuild Jewry in America, we will die as a people! We must replace the treasures we have lost. *(Malter has a heart attack. This can be shown or implied ... )*

REUVEN. My father had a heart attack. He was rushed to Brooklyn Memorial Hospital and, thank God, was soon in stable condition. He was so weak, however, he would have to spend more than a month in the hospital recovering. That same day Reb Saunders called me.

SAUNDERS. *(On phone.)* How can you live alone?

YOUNG REUVEN. *(On phone.)* I'll be all right.

SAUNDERS. *(On phone.)* It is a terrible thing for a boy your age to be left alone. We will put another bed in Daniel's room. You will sleep there. It is done.

YOUNG REUVEN. *(On phone.)* I don't want to be in the way.

SAUNDERS. *(On phone.)* Please. It will be a blessing to help my son's friend.

REUVEN. My father told me it would be wise to accept the offer.

YOUNG REUVEN. *(On phone.)* Thank you. My father and I are very grateful for your generosity.

REUVEN. So, on the first day of July, 1945, I left my house and moved into the Saunders' home. *(Young Reuven crosses the gulf between his father's study and Saunders' study, where Saunders and Danny wait for him and welcome him to their home. Blackout.)*

# ACT TWO

## Scene 1

## Explosions

*Music plays. Reuven enters.*

REUVEN. *(To us.)* I remember in grade school there was a sign above the chalkboard: *Reden iz Zilber; Shveigen iz Gold.* *(Translating.)* Speech is Silver, Silence is Golden. Even when I was six or seven, I found this proverb deeply suspect. Now it seemed utterly ridiculous. *(The boys enter and go to Saunders' office.)* The entire month I lived with the Saunders family that summer before college, I never heard Danny and his father say more than "pass the salt" to each other, except when we studied Talmud. They seemed almost physically incapable of talking. *(Saunders enters.)* Reb Saunders seemed almost in mourning and walked around the house stooped, as through there were literally a great weight on his shoulders. From time to time he'd begin to weep, out of nowhere, and leave the room, only to return a few minutes later as if nothing had happened. His followers came day and night to seek his advice and tell more tales of loss and horror from Europe.

SAUNDERS. ...it is impossible, inconceivable. Each day, each day we receive news of greater and greater devastation. The losses are immeasurable.

YOUNG REUVEN. My father says the same thing. He says American Jewry is all that is left now to carry on.

SAUNDERS. It is God's will. We must wait, and pray.

YOUNG REUVEN. A lot of people now are saying that it is time that Palestine became a Jewish homeland. They say that the time for waiting and praying is passed and not —

37

SAUNDERS. *(Quiet at first, but quickly furious.)* Who says this? Who are these people? *Apikorsim! Goyim!* Ben Gurion and his *goyim* will build *Eretz Yisroel*? They will bring Torah into this land? *Goyishkeit* they will bring into the land, not Torah!!! And where is the Messiah? Should we forget completely about the Messiah? For this six million were slaughtered? Who says *we* should build *Eretz Yisroel*? Who? I'll tell you who. *Apikorsim!! Jewish goyim!!! (He leaves. Door slams. The boys are left alone in his study.)*

YOUNG REUVEN. *(Hushed, to Danny.)* My God, I didn't know he felt that way about Zionism.

DANNY. *(Frustrated, embarrassed, angry, confused ... )* My father takes God and Torah absolutely seriously. In his eyes a secular Jewish state is a terrible sacrilege.

YOUNG REUVEN. Well, my father takes God and Torah —

DANNY. *(Barely restraining himself.)* Zionists like Herzl and Ben Gurion are not real Jews to him. They are not followers of the commandments. They are *apikorsim*. They are contaminated, and so is Zionism. It's that simple to him. Don't ever mention Zionism in front of him again.

YOUNG REUVEN. I won't, believe me.

DANNY. You've got be careful what you say around here.

YOUNG REUVEN. I guess so.

DANNY. You've got to be careful what you think around here!

YOUNG REUVEN. Danny...?

DANNY. *(Bursting.)* You have no idea what it's like! *(Beat. Finding the words.)* Imagine being locked in a cell where you can see the whole world and everything you want is right outside the window, but you're not allowed to look or think or move and you are supposed to stay right there, trapped, just like that, your whole life. Do you have any idea what that feels like? *(Beat.)*

YOUNG REUVEN. No. *(Beat.)* How could I? *(Beat.)*

DANNY. Listen, I love my father. I do. I don't know what he's trying to do with this silence he's established between us, but I think he's a great man and I respect him and trust him completely, which is why I think I can live with the silence. And I pity him, too. He's trapped. He was born trapped. *But I can't stay trapped.* I can't. *(Beat. With meaning.)* And I won't.

YOUNG REUVEN. *(Amazed.)* You mean you'll refuse...? After

six generations?

DANNY.  My brother could take his place. Don't you think?

YOUNG REUVEN.  Levi?

DANNY.  He's a good kid. He's quiet, but he's bright. He could make a fine *tzaddik*.

YOUNG REUVEN.  Sure, I guess, but —

DANNY.  Don't worry, it won't be for a while. Not while I still live at home. But someday ...

YOUNG REUVEN.  What will you do?

DANNY.  I don't know. But I've got to be able to breathe. How can I ask questions and then ignore the answers? How can I read Freud and then ignore everything I've learned?

YOUNG REUVEN.  My God Danny ...

DANNY.  Don't worry, I'll work it out. It's like Talmud, when the commentaries contradict each other. There is always a way to reconciling the different points of view, somehow. I've just got to figure it out ...

## Scene 2

## Hirsch

REUVEN.  The rest of that summer Danny and I spent almost all our time together, studying Talmud or at the library, where he continued with Freud and I continued with symbolic logic. I also followed the news from Europe carefully. With each news report, I felt more and more compelled to do something. Although I could not conceive yet of what that "something" might be ... In August my father moved home, and a few weeks later Danny and I started our first year at Hirsch College. *(Bell rings. Upbeat music plays. The boys enter, now a bit older, books in hand perhaps ... )* By the end of the first month I was having the time of my life, and Danny was thoroughly, thoroughly miserable.

DANNY.  *(Mid-rant.)* Experimental psychology!?!? Rats and mazes?!?!

REUVEN.  Danny's psychology professor was Dr. Nathan

Appleman.

DANNY. This is what I've been waiting for all this time?! Rats and mazes?!?!

REUVEN. He had an intense dislike for psychoanalysis in general —

DANNY. What has that got to do with the human mind, with the unconscious, with Freud?!?

REUVEN. And Freud in particular.

DANNY. It's ridiculous!

YOUNG REUVEN. Why don't you talk to him about it?

DANNY. About what? About *Freud?* The one time I mentioned Freud all I got out of Appleman was that psychoanalysis was related to psychology as magic was related to science. *(Reuven speaks as Appleman, as Danny perhaps speaks simultaneously or speaks quietly under or mouths the words:)*

REUVEN/APPLEMAN. "Dogmatic Freudians are interested solely in confirming hypothetical theories through a subjective process of analogy and induction, and make no attempt to achieve objective results through proven scientific testing methodologies."

DANNY. That was my introduction to experimental psychology. I've been running rats through mazes ever since!

YOUNG REUVEN. Was he right?

DANNY. Was who right?

YOUNG REUVEN. Appleman.

DANNY. About what?

YOUNG REUVEN. About Freudians being dogmatic.

DANNY. What followers of a genius aren't dogmatic, for heaven's sake?! Of course they're dogmatic. And they have plenty to be dogmatic about.

YOUNG REUVEN. Why?

DANNY. Because Freud was a genius!

YOUNG REUVEN. Okay, okay. So why don't you talk to Appleman about it?

DANNY. And tell him what? Freud's a genius? I hate experimental psychology?! You know what he said today?

REUVEN/APPLEMAN. *(With Danny under, as before.)* "Psychology may be regarded as a science only to the degree to which its hypotheses are subjected to laboratory testing and subsequent mathematization."

DANNY. Mathematization! You should be taking this course, not me.

YOUNG REUVEN. He's right, you know.

DANNY. Who's right?

YOUNG REUVEN. Appleman. If Freudians aren't willing to test their theories under laboratory conditions they *are* being dogmatic.

DANNY. Whose side are you on?

YOUNG REUVEN. Yours. It's just that he happens to be right about this. The rules of inductive logic state —

DANNY. I don't need a lecture on inductive logic! I need a teacher who is interested in human beings. What do rats have to do with the human mind?

YOUNG REUVEN. I don't know, but I'll bet Appleman does. Why don't you *ask* him?

DANNY. How is that going to help? What's he going to tell me?

YOUNG REUVEN. I don't know! I'm not him! But that's why we have teachers. *Talk to him.* Not everyone answers questions with silence! *(Danny looks hard at Reuven like he was slapped. Reuven realizes what he said.)* I'm sorry. I didn't mean ...

DANNY. I better go.

YOUNG REUVEN. Danny, wait. I didn't mean —

DANNY. Look, I know you hate my father, and I won't —

YOUNG REUVEN. I don't hate him. I just don't understand him. *(The bell rings.)*

DANNY. I better get going. I'm going to be late for Appleman. More rats!

## Scene 3

### Worthy of Rest

REUVEN. So it went. I found school fascinating and enlightening, and Danny found it frustrating and stifling, even though his brilliance in Rav Gershenson's Talmud class vaulted him to almost mythic status and he quickly became a leader among the Hasidic students.

Overall the Hasidim had always got along with the other Jews at Hirsch pretty well, but now a major rift was beginning over one overpowering issue: Zionism. It wasn't just our fathers who were at odds. The split divided both students and faculty, and feelings ran deep on both sides. The Hasidim, like Danny's father, saw Zionism as a socialist, secularist, sacrilegious movement. The very idea of a Jewish state established by non-religious Jews was unimaginable to them. Whereas passionate Zionists, like my father, saw a Jewish homeland in Palestine as the only hope for a devastated and embattled people. *(Late night. Malter at his desk with Reuven.)*

MALTER.  Did you know that on December 17, 1942, Mr. Eden got up in front of the House of Commons and gave the complete details of the Nazi plan to massacre the Jewish population of Europe? It was not a secret. There were protests, petitions, letters, and yet no practical measures were taken. None. They simply didn't care enough to do anything. They let a few Jews in and then closed their doors. Also in America, yes, they cared, but not enough. The world closed its doors to us. And now they would deny us Palestine as well. What a world this is. What an insane world …

YOUNG REUVEN.  You're working too hard. You'll make yourself sick again.

MALTER.  I'm fine …

YOUNG REUVEN.  Does Dr. Grossman know you're working like this?

MALTER.  Dr. Grossman worries too much. That's his job.

YOUNG REUVEN.  Are you going for another checkup soon?

MALTER.  Don't worry, I'm fine … *(Reuven hovers and looks worried as he serves tea and snacks.)*

YOUNG REUVEN.  I just wish you'd take it a little easy.

MALTER.  *(Blowing up, with great passion and frustration.)* This is a time to take things easy?!? The Haganah and Irgun boys who are dying, are they taking it easy!? This is the time for action. All the senseless slaughter will have meaning only if something lasting can emerge from the ashes. We must succeed in the creation of the Jewish homeland! It is the only hope for our people. *(Lengthy pause. When he speaks again he is fully in control again and speaks with love, passion, and compassion.)* Reuven, listen to me: Do you know what the rabbis tell us God said to Moses when he was about to die?

YOUNG REUVEN. No.

MALTER. God said: "You have toiled and labored, and now you are worthy of rest." *Worthy of rest.* We do not live forever. We live less than the time it takes to blink an eye. So then *why* do we live? What value is there to our life if it is nothing more than the blink of an eye? The blink of an eye is nothing. But *the eye that blinks,* now that just might be something. The *span* of a life is nothing, but the man who *lives* may be something if he fills his life with meaning. Meaning is not automatically given to life. We must *choose.* And if we choose to fill our lives with meaning, then perhaps when we die we too will be worthy of rest. And that is why I am doing what I am doing. You understand?

YOUNG REUVEN. *Abba ...*

MALTER. Don't worry, I am not going to die for a very long time. Between you and Dr. Grossman I'll live to be 112 — and three months. But I must do these things or my life would be meaningless. Merely to live, to exist — what sense is there in that? A fly also lives.

YOUNG REUVEN. I understand, *Abba. (Beat.)* And I respect your choices.

MALTER. You respect — ? *(Beat.)* Thank you, Reuven. That means a great deal to me. Thank you. *(Beat.)* Now listen a moment, would you? I want to read you the end of the speech I'm working on for the rally at Madison Square Garden. I want to know what you think of it.

YOUNG REUVEN. All right. *(During the speech the lights shift and Malter's voice begins to come from the radio at the rally. We hear the crowd, applause, cheering, music under ... We hear the speech continue. It is a big success ... )*

MALTER. My friends, we now have it in our grasp to bring the long, bitter centuries of exile to an end. Again and again we have sought acceptance in the lands where we settled. Again and again we were rejected and cast out. And what we have seen in our time is the final casting out of the Jews, the burning of an entire civilization. All of us stood as onlookers to that burning. We might absolve ourselves of our guilt as bystanders by saying no one could have anticipated such an evil. But we will never be able to rid ourselves of future guilt if we stand by and do nothing while our brothers and sisters in Palestine fight to establish a Jewish state. We must say to ourselves: Never again will Jews be bystanders to evil. Never again will Jews be bystanders to such a destruction. Never again will Jews be bystanders while other Jews struggle against oppression. Never again! Never again!! Never again!!! Never again!!!!

## Scene 4

## The Split

*Coming out of the energy at the end of the speech, music still playing underneath, this drives directly into the next section ...*

REUVEN. The speech was an enormous success! The Garden had been filled, with more than two thousand people outside listening to the speech over loudspeakers! It was broadcast nationally, reprinted in its entirety in the Yiddish press and even the New York *Times* reprinted lengthy sections. The next day at Hirsch I was something of a celebrity. *(Reuven is at school. Danny appears quickly, grabs Reuven, and takes him aside somewhere. When they are alone ... )*

DANNY. *(Terse and to the point.)* You are excommunicated from my family. My father heard your father's speech. I am not to see you, talk to you, be within four feet of you, ever again. If I don't obey he will remove me from Hirsch and send me away for my rabbinical ordination, no college education, no psychology, no nothing.

YOUNG REUVEN. That's crazy. That's totally insane.

DANNY. It's done. There is nothing I can do. I'm sorry, Reuven, I'm very sorry.

YOUNG REUVEN. That's it? That's all?

DANNY. I won't disobey my father. I can't.

YOUNG REUVEN. Fine. Fine. Good-bye.

DANNY. Good-bye. *(Danny leaves. The scene shifts instantly to Malter's and Saunders' studies. Both boys angrily confront their fathers, each in their own way ... The lines come in pairs, overlapping but not necessarily in unison.)*

YOUNG REUVEN. *(Simultaneously.)* It's not fair!

DANNY. *(Simultaneously.)* It's not fair!

MALTER. *(Simultaneously.)* I am sorry.

SAUNDERS. *(Simultaneously.)* I am sorry.

YOUNG REUVEN. *(Simultaneously.)* I don't understand ...

DANNY. *(Simultaneously.)* I don't understand ...

YOUNG REUVEN. *(Continuing.)* He let us be friends all these years, he let me live with them.

DANNY. *(Continuing.)* It was his father's words, not his. The son is not the father.

YOUNG REUVEN. *(Simultaneously.)* I don't understand ...

DANNY. *(Simultaneously.)* I don't understand ...

MALTER. *(Simultaneously.)* Your friendship was private. My Zionism is public. I cannot allow this friendship to continue in public.

SAUNDERS. *(Simultaneously.)* Your friendship was private. His Zionism is public. He cannot allow this friendship to continue in public.

MALTER. I am deeply sorry.

DANNY. Please...!

SAUNDERS. This discussion is over

DANNY. Please, *tatte!*

YOUNG REUVEN. He's a fanatic, *Abba!*

DANNY. Please.

SAUNDERS. It is done! *(Danny leaves.)*

YOUNG REUVEN. He's a fanatic!

MALTER. The fanaticism of men like Reb Saunders kept us alive for two thousand years of exile. If the Jews in Palestine have an ounce of that same fanaticism and use it wisely, we'll soon have a Jewish state! *(Heart attack. Again, it can be shown or implied.)*

REUVEN. That night my father had a second heart attack, was in critical condition for three days, and spent the next two months in the hospital. Now, for the first time in my life I was totally alone. *(Music grows, expands, fills the space as Reuven sits alone, isolated, cut off. This should continue as long as it can be maintained. The music becomes as loud as can be tolerated ... and then ends abruptly. Young Reuven is entirely alone. Reuven speaks eventually from away, out of the light, quiet, separate. He is prodding himself, encouraging himself, prompting himself to learn, to understand, to grow ... )*

## Scene 5

### Alone

*Beat. Silence. Beat. To himself.*

YOUNG REUVEN. It's not fair.

REUVEN. Life is not fair. Where is it written that life should be fair? *Dos leben is schver.* Life is tough.

YOUNG REUVEN. Silence is ugly. It's cruel. It's death. I hate it.

REUVEN. Silence is nothing, nothing at all. It's an unwritten sheet, a blank canvas. For you to fill ...

YOUNG REUVEN. I can't.

REUVEN. Why not?

YOUNG REUVEN. I'm all alone.

REUVEN. *Es lacht zich alain, un es vaint zich alain.* One laughs alone and weeps alone. We're *all* all alone.

YOUNG REUVEN. I don't know what to do.

REUVEN. Yes. You do. What draws you? What fills *you?*

YOUNG REUVEN. Talmud.

REUVEN. Then put your energy there. *Klop zich nicht dine kop in vant.* Don't beat your head against a wall. If one door is locked, go through one that is open. *(Reuven slowly, carefully opens a Talmud. Music plays gently underneath ... )* So I did. I threw myself into the study of Talmud, and soon found a sense of peace and purpose in this study that I had never found in mathematics, no matter how much it fascinated me. I saw for the first time that the Talmud had been created by Jews across the ages to deal with the ever-shifting crises and conflicts that arose during their day, and that now, through it, I might begin to find answers to the seemingly impossible questions that I was confronting, that all Jews were confronting after the devastation in Europe. I began to see the study of Talmud not as an end in itself, but as a means to a much larger end. And I began to see new possibilities for myself, a new path unfolding. In this, I found the strength to endure the silence that hung in my house during the long months of my father's recuperation, and my continuing excommunication from Danny. *(Music plays. Reuven becomes Jack Rose, a wealthy, portly, secular Jew. Malter enters and joins him.)*

## Scene 6

### A Religious Renaissance

REUVEN/JACK. ... and don't be such a *schmo* David, take a break, maybe a little vacation.

MALTER. When Israel is a fact, not a fantasy, there will be time for —

REUVEN/JACK. You're not the Messiah, you know. It's not your responsibility.

MALTER. That is a great relief to me. Thank you, Jack.

YOUNG REUVEN. *(Entering.)* Hello, *Abba*. Hello, Mr. Rose. *(To his father.)* How are you feeling?

MALTER. Very well, thank you.

REUVEN/JACK. *(Pinching his cheek.)* How's the *yeshiva bocher?* Getting good marks?

YOUNG REUVEN. I'm doing pretty well, thanks.

REUVEN/JACK. Working too hard, like your old man?

YOUNG REUVEN. *(Unsure how to answer such a stupid question ... )* Umm, I don't think so.

REUVEN/JACK. Good. Don't. Live a little. You're only young once. *(Checks his watch.)* Oh, hell, I gotta run. Take care of yourself, David, and *(Referring to a check.)* don't spend it all in one place. *(He laughs at his joke.).* Take care, Reuven, and take good care of your father. Don't let him work himself to death.

YOUNG REUVEN. Yes, I won't. Thanks. *(Jack leaves, chuckling ...)*

MALTER. *(Looking after Jack. Beat. Trying to find a delicate but true way to put it.)* He's a unique individual.

YOUNG REUVEN. I've never understood how you and he have remained friends all these years.

MALTER. And why should we not be friends?

YOUNG REUVEN. Well ... don't you disagree on just about everything?

MALTER. Friendship is not based only on similarities of opinion.

YOUNG REUVEN. I know, but —

MALTER. Differences of opinion should never be allowed to destroy a friendship. I am surprised that you of all people have not realized that yet.

YOUNG REUVEN. I do know that, *Abba.* But Jack Rose?

MALTER. Yes, Jack Rose. He is a good man, a good father, and a good friend. *(Showing the check.)* Not to mention he just gave me one thousand dollars for the Jewish National Fund.

YOUNG REUVEN. You're kidding?

MALTER. And he just joined a synagogue!

YOUNG REUVEN. Jack Rose? The Jack Rose who was just here?

MALTER. The same.

YOUNG REUVEN. I have a hard time seeing Jack Rose in a synagogue.

MALTER. He told me he joined not for himself, but for his children and grandchildren. And they say this is happening all over America now. A religious renaissance, some are calling it.

YOUNG REUVEN. I don't envy his rabbi.

MALTER. Why not? This is cause for celebration. American Jews are returning to the synagogues.

YOUNG REUVEN. God help us if the congregations fill up with all Jack Roses.

MALTER. They will fill up with Jack Roses and it will be the task of the rabbis to educate them. You see? That is what you would be up against if you were to become a rabbi.

YOUNG REUVEN. *(A brief beat. Taking a plunge ... )* You mean,

48

*when* I become a rabbi.

MALTER. *If* you become a rabbi.

YOUNG REUVEN. But *Abba* —

MALTER. You are young yet. There is time to decide such things.

YOUNG REUVEN. But rabbis are needed now more than ever. You say that all the time. That our treasures must be restored, and that the best hope lies here in America.

MALTER. Yes, I know, but —

YOUNG REUVEN. I think I could be helpful to our people, *Abba.* I want to teach, but I also want to be helpful to people in their real lives, in their times of need.

MALTER. I understand that, however —

YOUNG REUVEN. Are you the only one allowed to act on his beliefs, to fill his life with meaning?

MALTER. Ah. *(Beat.)* Ah, well. You would have been a fine professor. I would have enjoyed that.

YOUNG REUVEN. I know what I need to do. I've given it a lot of thought, believe me.

MALTER. *(A little smile.)* Even with a synagogue full of Jack Roses?

YOUNG REUVEN. Even then. God help me.

MALTER. You are a fine young man, Reuven, and you'll make a fine rabbi. I am only sorry that your mother could not — I hope you know, will always know, that I am very, very proud of you.

REUVEN. Meanwhile Arabs attacked Jewish settlements in Galilee, the Negev and around Jerusalem. But as the spring wore on, and the fighting escalated in Palestine, fighting actually cooled within the school as once again Jews were being killed. In May, when the State of Israel was officially proclaimed, my father and I wept with joy and relief and exhaustion. But then began the invasions by the surrounding nations. And when word came back that a recent graduate of Hirsch, a brilliant student named Ira Kohn, had been killed in Israel, all fighting within the school suddenly stopped. Israel was now a fact, and Jews were once again united, at least for the moment, against common enemies. *(Beat.)* My father and I spent most of the summer in a small cabin in Peekskill, New York, reading, writing, and studying Talmud. It was a peaceful time and the rest did us both good. The first day back at Hirsch was a beautiful fall morning.

# Scene 7

## The Reconciliation

*Young Reuven sits reading on a bench outside of Hirsch. Danny approaches carefully.*

DANNY. Good book? *(Beat.)* Hello. *(Beat.)* How are you?

YOUNG REUVEN. You're actually talking to me, aren't you?

DANNY. The ban has been lifted.

YOUNG REUVEN. I'm kosher again?

DANNY. I'm sorry.

YOUNG REUVEN. And that's it? That's all?

DANNY. I did what I had to do.

YOUNG REUVEN. *Had* to do?

DANNY. What I *chose* to do.

YOUNG REUVEN. I see. *(Beat.)*

DANNY. So, are we still friends?

YOUNG REUVEN. I needed you, and you ... You didn't even fight him on this, did you?

DANNY. Reuven. Are we still friends?

YOUNG REUVEN. No. Yes. I don't know. *(He hits him with his book. Danny hits him with his hat. They hit each other for while, then finally laugh. Or something like that ... The tension is broken. They smile.)* Hello.

DANNY. Hello.

YOUNG REUVEN. Hi.

DANNY. How are you?

YOUNG REUVEN. Fine.

DANNY. How's your father? I heard he was sick. I wanted —

YOUNG REUVEN. I know. Thanks. He's already working too hard, again.

DANNY. Of course.

YOUNG REUVEN. And how is your family?

DANNY. They're all fine. The same.

YOUNG REUVEN. Your father?

DANNY. The same. *(Beat.)* You've been very impressive in Rav Gershenson's Talmud class.

YOUNG REUVEN. Thanks.

DANNY. And I've heard talk.

YOUNG REUVEN. About what?

DANNY. About you becoming a rabbi. Is it true?

YOUNG REUVEN. Yes.

DANNY. What about symbolic logic?

YOUNG REUVEN. It'll have to wait. There's too much to do that can't wait.

DANNY. I see. *(Beat.)* Reuven? I have something I have to tell you.

YOUNG REUVEN. What? It can't be worse then not talking.

DANNY. I can't wait anymore either ... I'm leaving.

YOUNG REUVEN. What?

DANNY. I'm transferring from Hirsch. To study psychology.

YOUNG REUVEN. *(Stunned.)* When?

DANNY. Next year. I am applying to schools now.

YOUNG REUVEN. Can't you study psychology here?

DANNY. Not the kind I want. This was all Dr. Appleman's idea, actually.

YOUNG REUVEN. What?!

DANNY. Yes. I finally took your advice. He is really a very fine man. But experimental psychology is not what I want to study. I want to work with people, not rats.

YOUNG REUVEN. Have you told your father yet?

DANNY. No. Not yet.

YOUNG REUVEN. Well, let me know when you do, so I can remember to be out of town that day.

DANNY. Maybe I'll come with you. *(Beat.)* Have you told your father yet? About being a rabbi.

YOUNG REUVEN. Yes.

DANNY. What did he say?

YOUNG REUVEN. He's disappointed I won't be a professor, but he respects my decision.

DANNY. I see. *(Brief pause.)* I can't get over you becoming a rabbi.

YOUNG REUVEN.  I can't get over you becoming a psychologist. *(Beat.)*
DANNY.  It's a funny world, isn't it?


## Scene 8

## Listening to Silence


REUVEN.  So more than a year of silence ended. Soon we were back to our old routine of meeting in the mornings, riding the trolley to school, eating lunch together and taking walks at night after our studies. *(The boys walk at night.)* I avoided seeing his father, though. The silence between him and Danny continued. And although Danny and I rarely talked about it directly, he would sometimes, for no apparent reason, grow strangely thoughtful and distant, and I felt sure that at these moments he was thinking about his father. *(Beat.)* It turned out I was only half right about that ... *(In a park, late at night. It is quiet; they are alone. They play catch, maybe. The scene is gentle, unhurried ... Beat.)*
DANNY.  *(Beat.)* You can learn to live with it, you know.
YOUNG REUVEN.  Live with what?
DANNY.  Silence. It's not so bad, really.
YOUNG REUVEN.  You're kidding?
DANNY.  No. I'm not. I've found ... I've found that you can listen to silence. *(Beat.)* And more than that. I've found it begins to ... to talk to you.
YOUNG REUVEN.  What do you mean?
DANNY.  You can hear silence, Reuven. It has a quality and a dimension all its own. It talks to me. I feel myself alive in it. It talks. And I can hear it. *(Reuven looks at him in amazement.)* You don't understand that, do you?
YOUNG REUVEN.  What do you mean, it talks to you?
DANNY.  It speaks to me. It has a strange, beautiful texture. And it doesn't always talk. Sometimes it cries, and I can hear such pain

52

in it. It hurts to listen to. But now I don't have a choice ...
YOUNG REUVEN.   You know, you should get a girlfriend. Seriously, I'm getting worried about you. I don't think you should be going around, "listening to silence." And a girl is a great tonic for a suffering soul.
DANNY.   My wife has been chosen for me.
YOUNG REUVEN.   What? You're kidding.
DANNY.   No, it's an old Hasidic custom.
YOUNG REUVEN.   Oh, my God.
DANNY.   It is just going to make everything harder.
YOUNG REUVEN.   You mean ...
DANNY.   When I leave. It's not just my family involved. *(The scene instantly cross-fades to Reuven with his father in his study ... )*
MALTER.   When did Daniel tell you all this?
YOUNG REUVEN.   He's talked about being a psychologist for a long time.
MALTER.   And you never told me?
YOUNG REUVEN.   It was a secret between us.
MALTER.   Does he know what pain this will cause his father?
YOUNG REUVEN.   He dreads telling him.
MALTER.   Reuven, ask Daniel to come see me. I want to talk to him.
REUVEN.   So I did. *(The scene instantly cross-fades and Danny is there.)*
MALTER.   Do not be angry with Reuven for telling me about your decision. I think you'll remember that I have had practice keeping secrets. So, when will you tell your father?
DANNY.   Soon.
MALTER.   And there is a girl involved? *(Danny nods.)* You will refuse to marry this girl?
DANNY.   Yes.
MALTER.   And your father will have to explain it to her family and his followers? *(Danny nods.)* This will be a very ... uncomfortable situation. For you and your father.
DANNY.   Yes, I know.
MALTER.   You are determined not to take his place?
DANNY.   I am.
MALTER.   Then you must know exactly what you will tell him.

53

Think carefully. Think what he will be most concerned about after he hears of your decision. Do you understand, Danny? *(Danny nods.)* Daniel, you can hear silence? *(Danny looks to Reuven, back at Malter.)*

DANNY. Yes.

MALTER. You are not angry with your father?

DANNY. No.

MALTER. Do you understand what he is doing?

DANNY. No.

REUVEN. Danny heard from schools in the early spring. They all accepted him for the fall semester, and he chose Columbia. Still he hadn't told his father, who kept sending word through Danny that he wanted me to come study with them as I used to.

MALTER. What?

REUVEN. But I avoided it.

MALTER. You didn't tell me Reb Saunders has been asking to see you.

YOUNG REUVEN. He's been asking all along. He just asked again that I come over tomorrow, on Passover.

MALTER. Reuven, don't you see?

YOUNG REUVEN. What?

MALTER. When someone wants to speak to you, you must let them. Particularly if he has hurt you.

YOUNG REUVEN. He wants to study Talmud, *Abba.*

MALTER. You are sure?

YOUNG REUVEN. That's all we've ever done when I've gone over there.

MALTER. You only study Talmud? Have you forgotten so quickly?

YOUNG REUVEN. Oh my God. He wants to talk to Danny through me. Why didn't he tell me?

MALTER. He did tell you. You were not listening.

YOUNG REUVEN. It never occurred to me.

MALTER. Listen next time. Listen when someone speaks to you, no matter how they do it. If you are to be a rabbi, you must learn to listen behind the words, to the words that can't be spoken. Now go, call him ... And learn to listen more carefully ... *(Reuven leaves. To himself, after he is gone:)* My little rabbi.

REUVEN. And so, on Passover, I walked the five blocks to go and see Danny and Reb Saunders. As I walked slowly toward their house I thought of the first time Danny and I had walked there together, into that strange new world, and of everything that had happened since. I felt myself to be so very similar and so totally different from that sixteen-year-old boy ... (*Music plays. Reuven walks slowly. He enters Saunders' study, where he and Danny sit.*)


## Scene 9

## The End of Silence


SAUNDERS. *Nu*, finally, finally you come to see me, Reuven.

YOUNG REUVEN. I apologize.

SAUNDERS. You have become a man. The first day you sat here, you were only a boy. Now you are a man. My son, my Daniel, has also become a man. It is a great joy for a father to see his son suddenly a man. And what are your plans for the future, Reuven?

YOUNG REUVEN. I ... I am going to be a rabbi.

SAUNDERS. Ah, yes ... So, soon now my Daniel and his good friend begin to go different ways. You will go one way, and my son, my Daniel, he will — he will go another way. (*Reuven looks to Danny, who looks on, amazed. In response to their exchange:*) I know. I have known for a long time. Reuven, I want you to listen carefully to what I will tell you now.

REUVEN. His voice said "Reuven." His eyes said "Daniel." But still he talked to me ...

SAUNDERS. You may not understand it. And you may never stop hating me for what I have done. I know how you feel. I do not see it in your eyes? But, please, listen:

Reuven, the Master of the Universe blessed me with a brilliant son, a boy with a mind like a jewel. When my Daniel was four years old, I saw him reading a story from a book, and I was frightened. He did not read this story. He devoured it. It was a

55

sad story full of pain but my Daniel did not see that. He only saw, for the first time, the power of his mind and the tremendous memory he had. He was indifferent to the pain and I cried, I cried in my heart, "Master of the Universe, what have you done to me? A mind like this I need for a son? A heart I need for a son, a soul I need for a son, compassion, righteousness, mercy, strength to suffer, to carry pain, that I need from a son, not a mind without a soul!"

When I was young, Reuven, my father, may he rest in peace, *taught me with silence*. He did not trust words, words distort, words play tricks, they conceal the heart, the heart speaks through silence. He taught me that one learns of the pain of others by suffering one's own pain, by turning inside, by finding one's own soul. Of all people, he told me, a *tzaddik* must know of pain. Knowing pain destroys our self-pride, our arrogance, our indifference towards others. My Daniel understands this now. He understands it well.

Reuven, when I saw the mind my Daniel had, I knew what I must do to feed his soul, to force him to look inside himself. Yet I did not want to lose my son, my precious son whom I love as I love the Master of the Universe. I know he suffered. I know the pain, the loneliness he felt when I drew myself away from him. Once he laughed and said, "That man is so ignorant." I said, "Look into his soul and see the world through his eyes. You will know the pain he feels because of his ignorance and you will not laugh." He was bewildered and hurt. *But he learned.* He suffered and learned to hear the sufferings of others. *In the silence between us, he began to hear the world crying.*

Reuven, you and your father were a blessing to me. The Master of the Universe sent you to my son when he was ready to rebel. He sent you to listen to my son's words. I knew your soul was good and that you would be a good friend. I knew it that day my Daniel came home and told me he wanted to be your friend. Ah, you should have seen his eyes that day. You should have heard his voice. A thousand times I have thanked the Master of the Universe that he sent you to my son.

You think I was cruel. Perhaps. But he has learned. Let my Daniel become a psychologist. I know he wishes this. I don't see the books, the letters? I don't see his eyes? I do not hear his soul crying? For a long time I have known. Let my son become a psychologist. I have no more fear now. All his life he will be a *tzaddik. He will be a tzaddik for the world. And the world needs a tzaddik. (Pause. Daniel sits, weeping. Reb Saunders gathers his strength for a final effort, a shift from the years of silence. He speaks to his son:)* Daniel. My Daniel. When you go away, you will shave your beard and *payos? (Danny nods "yes.")* But you will live as a Jew, as an observer of the commandments?

DANNY. Yes.

SAUNDERS. Good. That is ... good. *(He turns to go. Turns back.)* My Daniel, *mein hertz,* forgive me ... for what I have done. A — a wiser father might have done differently. I ... I am not wise. *(They embrace.)* Today is Passover, the festival of freedom. Today my Daniel is free. *(He leaves.)*

REUVEN. Later that evening Danny and I went for long walk. *(They do. Music plays ... )* For hours we walked all over the neighborhood. We even spent some time sitting on the baseball diamond in my school yard where we had met nearly four years earlier. We didn't talk much. We just walked, enjoying a very wonderful kind of easy quiet between us, walking in silence and saying more with that silence than with a lifetime of words.

On the first Shabbat in June Reb Saunders told his followers of his son's decision. He told them that he respected his son's soul and mind — in that order — and that as he planned to remain a follower of the commandments, he therefore felt impelled to give him his blessing. The announcement was met with shocked dismay, and, quickly, acceptance, as Reb Saunders' decision was absolute. The *tzaddikate* would now be passed on to his younger son. A few days later he broke Danny's engagement in the same manner.

The reaction at Hirsch, once the news broke, lasted all of about ... two or three days. The non-Hasidic students talked about it for a day and forgot it. The Hasidic students sulked, scowled, glowered and then forgot it, too. Everyone was busy with final examinations. *(Music plays. Saunders enters and goes to his study to pray. Malter enters and goes to his study to study, much as they did at the beginning of the play. Young Reuven enters a*

57

*moment later into his father's study. A moment later Danny enters from behind his father's study, passing around it but not through it. He is wearing a new not-black suit, a skullcap or a hat and his payos are gone. He walks through the space to Malter's study.)*

DANNY. Hello.

YOUNG REUVEN. *(In response to his appearance.)* Hi.

MALTER. Hello, Daniel.

DANNY. I just came to say good-bye. And to thank you, Mr. Malter, for everything.

MALTER. It's been my pleasure. Good luck at Columbia. I hope you find what you are looking for.

DANNY. Thank you.

YOUNG REUVEN. Don't talk like he's going away forever. It's only across the bridge, it's not the Ukraine.

DANNY. My father asked if you would like to come study with us this week.

YOUNG REUVEN. Yes, of course. Tell him I will be glad to come. Any time.

DANNY. Good.

MALTER. What does he think of your new appearance?

DANNY. Not very much. He says he hardly recognizes me.

MALTER. Danny.

DANNY. Yes?

MALTER. May I ask you a question.

DANNY. Of course.

MALTER. When you have a son ... You will raise him as you were raised — in silence? *(Beat.)*

DANNY. If I cannot find another way. *(Malter and Reuven react with surprise.)* I've talked to my father about it, and he has told me a great deal about —

YOUNG REUVEN. You've talked to your father?

DANNY. Yes, we talk now. *(Beat.)* I must go. *(To Reuven.)* I'll see you on *Shabbos. (To Malter.)* And thank you again, Mr. Malter.

MALTER. Good-bye, Daniel. *(Music. Saunders and Malter read. Reuven watches Danny walk away.)*

REUVEN. In the Talmud there is an idea that occurs again and again in different ways. It is one of the cardinal principles of Talmud, an idea that is never challenged and resolves arguments.

When I was young, I never understood how it could be true. It was such a simple idea, yet it appeared at the most complex moments, when the conflicts and contradictions seemed almost impossible to reconcile.

It was on that Passover, in 1949, that I began — just began — to see how such an idea could be possible, even necessary. *(He looks up to where these words are written in Hebrew.)* It says: *Ayloo ve'ayloo deevray eloheem chaiyeem. (Translating.)* "*Both* these, *and* those, *are* the words of the living God." *(The banner is lit fully. All else fades away except the two boys. Lights fade ... )*

## End of Play

# PROPERTY LIST

Books (MALTER, SAUNDERS, YOUNG REUVEN)
Tea (YOUNG REUVEN, DANNY)
Snacks (YOUNG REUVEN)
Watch (JACK)
Check (MALTER)
Hat (DANNY)

# SOUND EFFECTS

Music
Street sounds, Brooklyn, 1944
Baseball game
Sirens
Hospital
Warped music
Men and boys speaking Yiddish
A crowd parting
Congregation at shul
Footsteps echoing
Shul service
Sounds of approval from a crowd
Radio news
Radio news of Hitler's death
Door slam
Bell
Crowd applauding and cheering

# NEW PLAYS

★ **THE CIDER HOUSE RULES, PARTS 1 & 2 by Peter Parnell, adapted from the novel by John Irving.** Spanning eight decades of American life, this adaptation from the Irving novel tells the story of Dr. Wilbur Larch, founder of the St. Cloud's, Maine orphanage and hospital, and of the complex father-son relationship he develops with the young orphan Homer Wells. "…luxurious digressions, confident pacing…an enterprise of scope and vigor…" –*NY Times.* "…The fact that I can't wait to see Part 2 only begins to suggest just how good it is…" –*NY Daily News.* "…engrossing…an odyssey that has only one major shortcoming: It comes to an end." –*Seattle Times.* "…outstanding…captures the humor, the humility…of Irving's 588-page novel…" –*Seattle Post-Intelligencer.* [9M 10W, doubling, flexible casting] PART 1 ISBN: 0-8222-1725-2 PART 2 ISBN: 0-8222-1726-0

★ **TEN UNKNOWNS by Jon Robin Baitz.** An iconoclastic American painter in his seventies has his life turned upside down by an art dealer and his ex-boyfriend. "…breadth and complexity…a sweet and delicate harmony rises from the four cast members…Mr. Baitz is without peer among his contemporaries in creating dialogue that spontaneously conveys a character's social context and moral limitations…" –*NY Times.* "…darkly funny, brilliantly desperate comedy…TEN UNKNOWNS vibrates with vital voices." –*NY Post.* [3M, 1W] ISBN: 0-8222-1826-7

★ **BOOK OF DAYS by Lanford Wilson.** A small-town actress playing St. Joan struggles to expose a murder. "…[Wilson's] best work since *Fifth of July*…An intriguing, prismatic and thoroughly engrossing depiction of contemporary small-town life with a murder mystery at its core…a splendid evening of theater…" –*Variety.* "…fascinating…a densely populated, unpredictable little world." –*St. Louis Post-Dispatch.* [6M, 5W] ISBN: 0-8222-1767-8

★ **THE SYRINGA TREE by Pamela Gien.** Winner of the 2001 Obie Award. A breathtakingly beautiful tale of growing up white in apartheid South Africa. "Instantly engaging, exotic, complex, deeply shocking…a thoroughly persuasive transport to a time and a place…stun[s] with the power of a gut punch…" –*NY Times.* "Astonishing…affecting …[with] a dramatic and heartbreaking conclusion…A deceptive sweet simplicity haunts THE SYRINGA TREE…" –*A.P.* [1W (or flexible cast)] ISBN: 0-8222-1792-9

★ **COYOTE ON A FENCE by Bruce Graham.** An emotionally riveting look at capital punishment. "The language is as precise as it is profane, provoking both troubling thought and the occasional cheerful laugh…will change you a little before it lets go of you." –*Cincinnati CityBeat.* "…excellent theater in every way…" –*Philadelphia City Paper.* [3M, 1W] ISBN: 0-8222-1738-4

★ **THE PLAY ABOUT THE BABY by Edward Albee.** Concerns a young couple who have just had a baby and the strange turn of events that transpire when they are visited by an older man and woman. "An invaluable self-portrait of sorts from one of the few genuinely great living American dramatists…rockets into that special corner of theater heaven where words shoot off like fireworks into dazzling patterns and hues." –*NY Times.* "An exhilarating, wicked…emotional terrorism." –*NY Newsday.* [2M, 2W] ISBN: 0-8222-1814-3

★ **FORCE CONTINUUM by Kia Corthron.** Tensions among black and white police officers and the neighborhoods they serve form the backdrop of this discomfiting look at life in the inner city. "The creator of this intense…new play is a singular voice among American playwrights…exceptionally eloquent…" –*NY Times.* "…a rich subject and a wise attitude." –*NY Post.* [6M, 2W, 1 boy] ISBN: 0-8222-1817-8

**DRAMATISTS PLAY SERVICE, INC.**
440 Park Avenue South, New York, NY 10016  212-683-8960  Fax 212-213-1539
postmaster@dramatists.com  www.dramatists.com